FOOTPRINTS *of* LIGHT

ANKITA SEN KUNDU

Illustrated by Ankita Sen Kundu

INDIA · SINGAPORE · MALAYSIA

ISBN
Domestic: 979-8-89133-726-8
International: 979-8-89277-830-5

In loving memory of

my grandmother Mrs. Induprabha Sen
and
my grandfather Dr. Jogesh Chandra Sen

I love you both very much.
Thank you for inspiring me.

CONTENTS

INTRODUCTION

A few years back, I started playing chess with my best friend. It was fun in the beginning, mostly because I was winning every day. Then, after a few weeks, I lost a game. Then I lost another game. Then I lost four games in a row. I was angry with myself, and I was heartbroken. I started thinking about it all day long, and somehow I kept losing again and again. Finally, I couldn't take it anymore and stopped playing with her altogether, giving her all sorts of excuses.

I carried on with my life, but I was sad most of the time because I was not proud of what I did and how I reacted. It continued like this for nearly six months until I forgot about it by engaging myself with more work.

A few months later, a similar incident happened again at work. I didn't get the promotion that I so badly wanted. I felt lost and shattered. I felt like leaving everything and running away. It really hit me hard. I had stopped smiling and talking to friends. My work efficiency started to decline. It was becoming very hard for me to get up every day for office. So, I took a long leave to stay away from everyone for a few days.

After being angry at the world for a very long time, I started questioning myself. During this alone time, free from all distractions, I began contemplating every aspect of my own life. What if I am the one responsible for everything that is happening to me and nobody else? How am I conducting myself? How am I behaving with myself? Why is it so difficult for me to be happy?

I started to see how a simple activity like playing a game and losing it, as well as not getting the promotion I so dearly wanted, was throwing me off the cliff in the exact same way. I clearly began to see how I always attached myself to these activities and worldly things, making them a part of my whole being, as if my life depended on them. I was strongly identifying myself with everything that was happening around me, and my vision of reality became completely blurred.

At that very moment, I realised that I was not alone in this mess. Each one of us is dragging ourselves into this mess knowingly or unknowingly. The fundamental problem for all of us is this: we are getting too identified with every single thing we encounter in our day-to-day lives, and that means a MILLION things. So, how can we ever be happy if there are a million probabilities for it? No way. We are very successfully planning on being sad, self-destructive, unhealthy, and thereby the worst people to be around. This has to stop right away.

I am trying hard to come out of this garbage bin I have kept myself in, and this book is a witness to my struggles. I earnestly request all my young readers to join me in this journey of healing by following the footprints left by great beings who have shown the light of wisdom to all humankind.

"Footprints of Light" is a small collection of some great learnings that I am following and will continue to follow for the rest of my life to become a truly joyful, peaceful, and loving human being. So, come, let's begin this joyride...

PART I

IGNORANCE

Chapter 1
ME

Picture 1: Hey, look, it's me. I am so awesome. I am so wealthy, beautiful, and intelligent. Wow... no one is better than me. I am the most powerful of all.

Picture 2: Hey, listen... I am a noticeable person in my country. They all respect me. I am big...

Picture 3: I can't find myself... oh, see... I am that small speck shown in my country. But that is a very small place compared to the world... huh...

Picture 4: Where am I? Can't find myself. Can't even see Earth. Oh, there I can see our Milky Way galaxy where Earth is located... but... Earth looks even smaller than a grain of sand compared to the rest of the cosmos...

Ohhh... so maybe I am not big... that was an illusion. In reality, I am small... smaller than I can ever imagine...

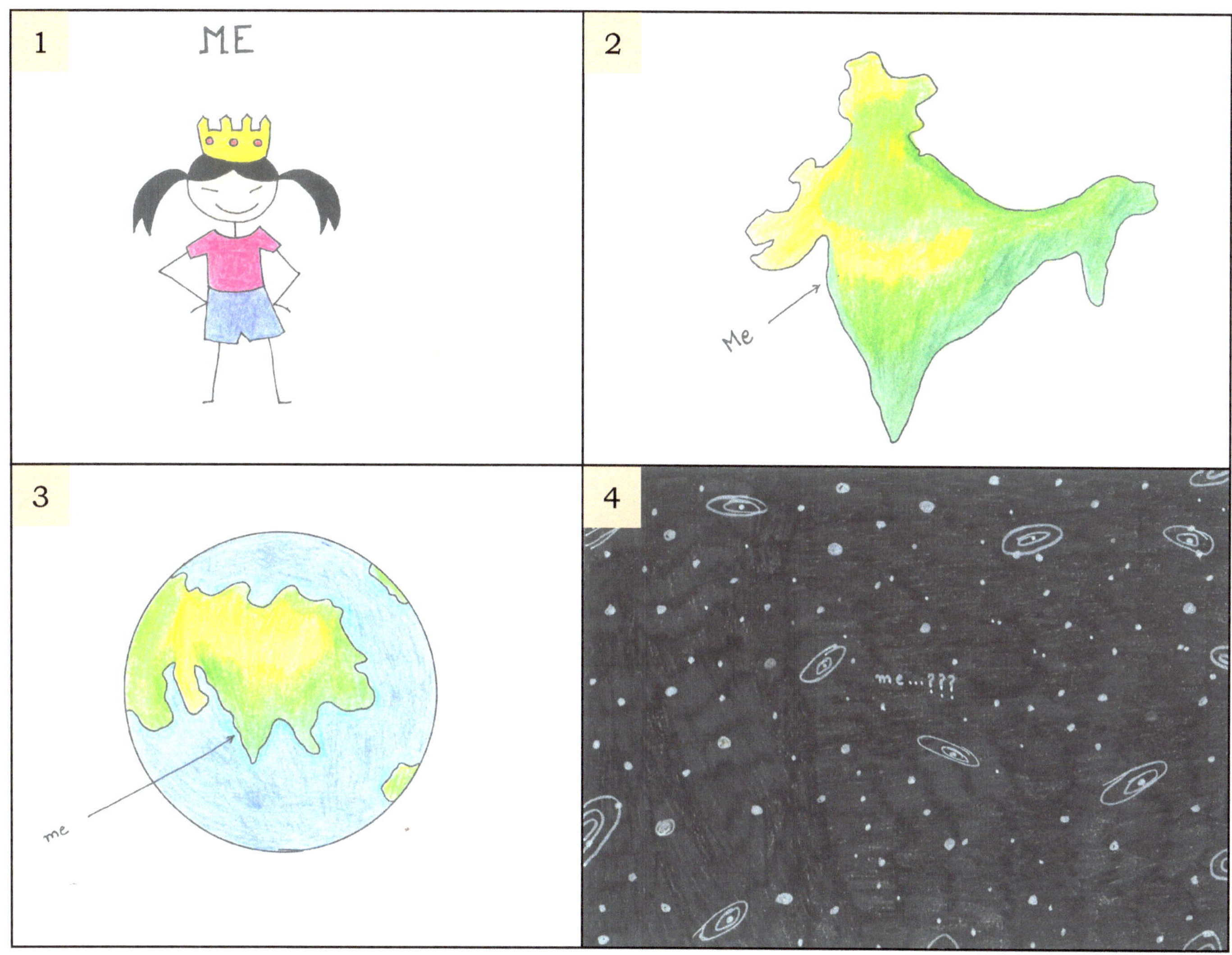
1
ME
2
Me
3
me
4
me...???

Chapter 2

ARE WE STILL...APE?

Hey, look at that girl; she is working very hard. But what for? Oh, look, she wants more money, a bigger home, fancy clothes... nice... But look, there is an ape. What's in its mind? It wants a bigger tree, more bananas, and a beautiful mate.

Hmm... why are her wants exactly similar to this ape? Aren't we humans more evolved? Aren't we more intelligent? Shouldn't we, as humans, strive for something more? Something a little more than physical pleasures? Think about it.

Are we Still . . . Ape ??
I have to work hard to gather more money!!
I have to build a bigger home!!
I want to buy more clothes!!
I want to collect more Bananas !!
I have to find a bigger tree to rest Under !!
I have to find a beauti-ful mate !!

Chapter 3
CHOICE

How we choose to live our lives must be our choice, right? Do you want to spend each day of your life crying and craving for a new toy, a new dress, or good food? Or do you want to spend each day doing something more meaningful, something that will give you peace, strength, and joy every day of your life? The choice is absolutely ours to make.

Note: *I have used this symbol to represent the Creator or the Almighty. It is a personal choice. It can be different for different people.*

CHOICE ?
I want a teddy!!
Will 9 ever get my teddy??
TODAY
TODAY
I want a chocolate!!
Will 9 ever get my chocolate??
TOMORROW
TOMORROW
I want a new dress !!
Will 9 ever get my new dress??
DAY AFTER TOMORROW
DAY AFTER TOMORROW

Chapter 4

ESSENCE OF LIFE

We often feel intimidated by highly intelligent people. We admire how amazingly their brains work, and we aspire to have the same in our lives. We work very hard to sharpen and train our brains, and our brains start to give excellent results. We achieve high marks, and perform well in school and work, and it feels like we are on top of the world.

However, after a few days, months, or years, our ego rises and takes over. We become super proud of ourselves, excessively arrogant, and extremely anxious about what to achieve next. Eventually, we become super stressed, depressed, and sad. Do you know why this happens?

Apart from intelligence, the brain is also capable of making us feel inferiority complex, fear, jealousy, and hatred. So, what can we do? We need to understand that the brain is just a machine, a tool for survival. It helps us live our lives by earning a living and keeping our bodies safe, but it is not 'The Life' itself.

Essence Of Life
Inferiority Complex
Fear
Jealousy
Hatred
Intelligence
Constituents of Human Brain
I want to be Intelligent
I want to be the best!
After a few days....
fear
Hatred
Anxiety
Then, one day she took the brave decision & chose over ...
She learned that brain is just a tool for survival & not the essence of her life...

Chapter 5

RIGHT OR WRONG

How can we determine what actions or things are right and what are wrong?

Before delving into understanding the right things, let's focus on the WRONG things. The things or actions that take away your peace or freedom are wrong. The actions or things that enslave you are wrong. But now the question is – freedom from what? Freedom from the constraints of external influence, from the artificial, money-centric world. Freedom is to be your authentic self, it is to become what you truly want to be, to create what you truly want to create and to learn what you genuinely desire. Freedom is to live life to the fullest without any fear.

Whatever actions compel you to deviate from this freedom and force you to live in fear, in doubt, in false assumptions about yourself and the world, are 'WRONG'. If you allow this 'WRONG' to dominate your mind, sadness is inevitable. However, if you can identify this 'WRONG' and strive to distance yourself from it, the 'RIGHT' will naturally take control, and happiness, peace, and victory will always prevail.

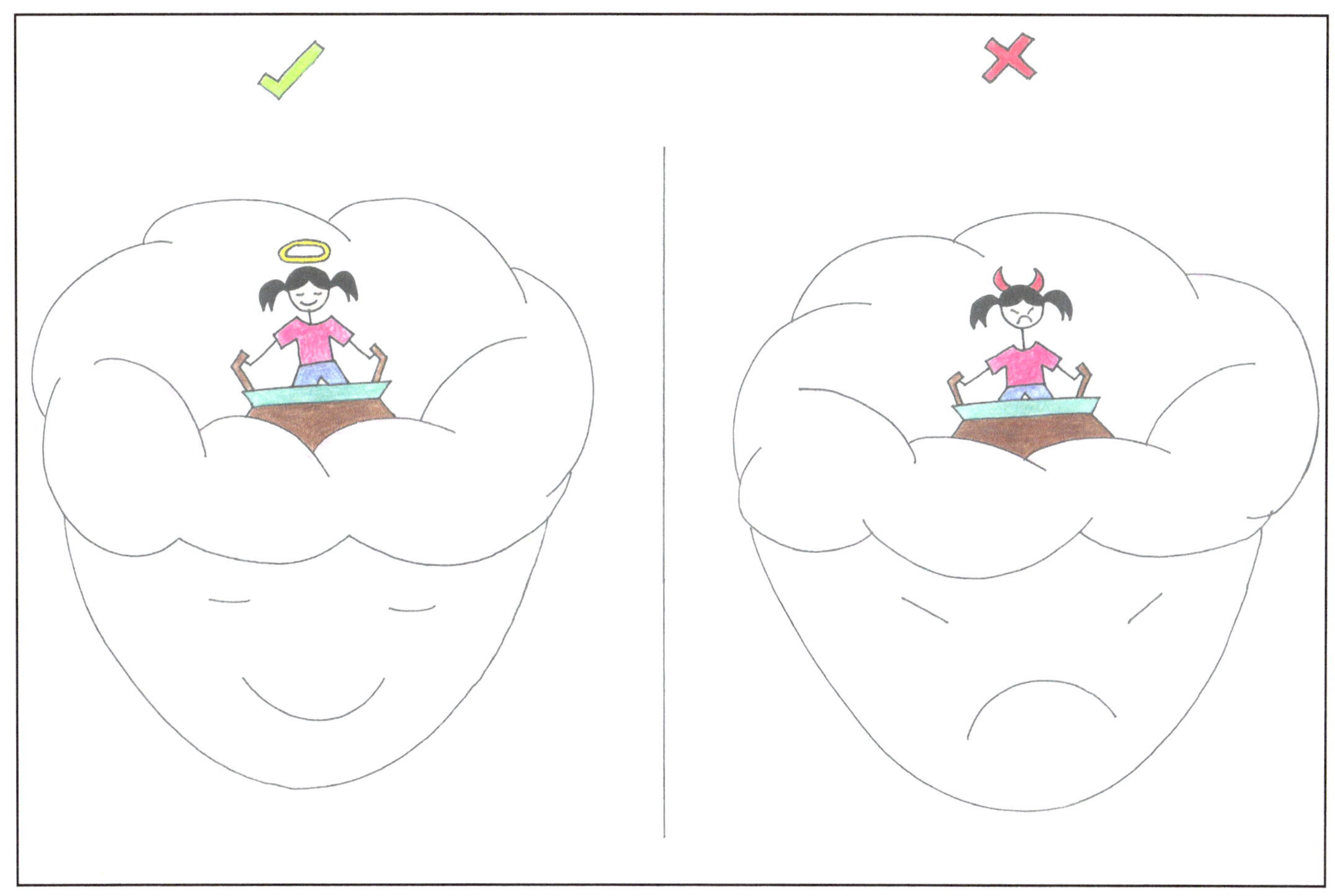

Chapter 6

WE TINY, OUR PROBLEMS TINIER

Have you ever wondered how tiny we are? Let me provide you with some perspective. The Sun weighs about 333,000 times as much as Earth. It is so large that about 1,300,000 planet Earths can fit inside of it. The solar system dwarfs Earth, being about 36 billion times its size. And do you know how small our Milky Way galaxy is, where our solar system resides? Our Milky Way galaxy is just one of approximately 100 billion galaxies in the universe.

So, given our tiny size and short lifespan, why waste it on fights and wars? No matter how hard we try to assert our egos, we will always remain tiny. This life, which is exceedingly small in comparison to the vast cosmos, should be spent in pure joy and amazement, by appreciating and taking care of this creation.

We can never fully experience all that our universe has to offer in this lifetime. Therefore, each day should be dedicated to recognizing that we are merely a small speck of life, and the powers governing this universe are unimaginably greater than us.

We tiny, Our Problems tinier.
1
#@#?
$#@!
2
3
Hey! I can't hear anybody!
4
Sun

PART 2

SCIENCE

Chapter 1

WHAT ARE WE MADE OF?

There are many theories that explain the workings of the world around us. One of these theories is 'String theory.' According to String theory, everything around us, including all physical things such as the air we breathe, the water we drink, and the food we eat, is composed of different vibrating energy strings.

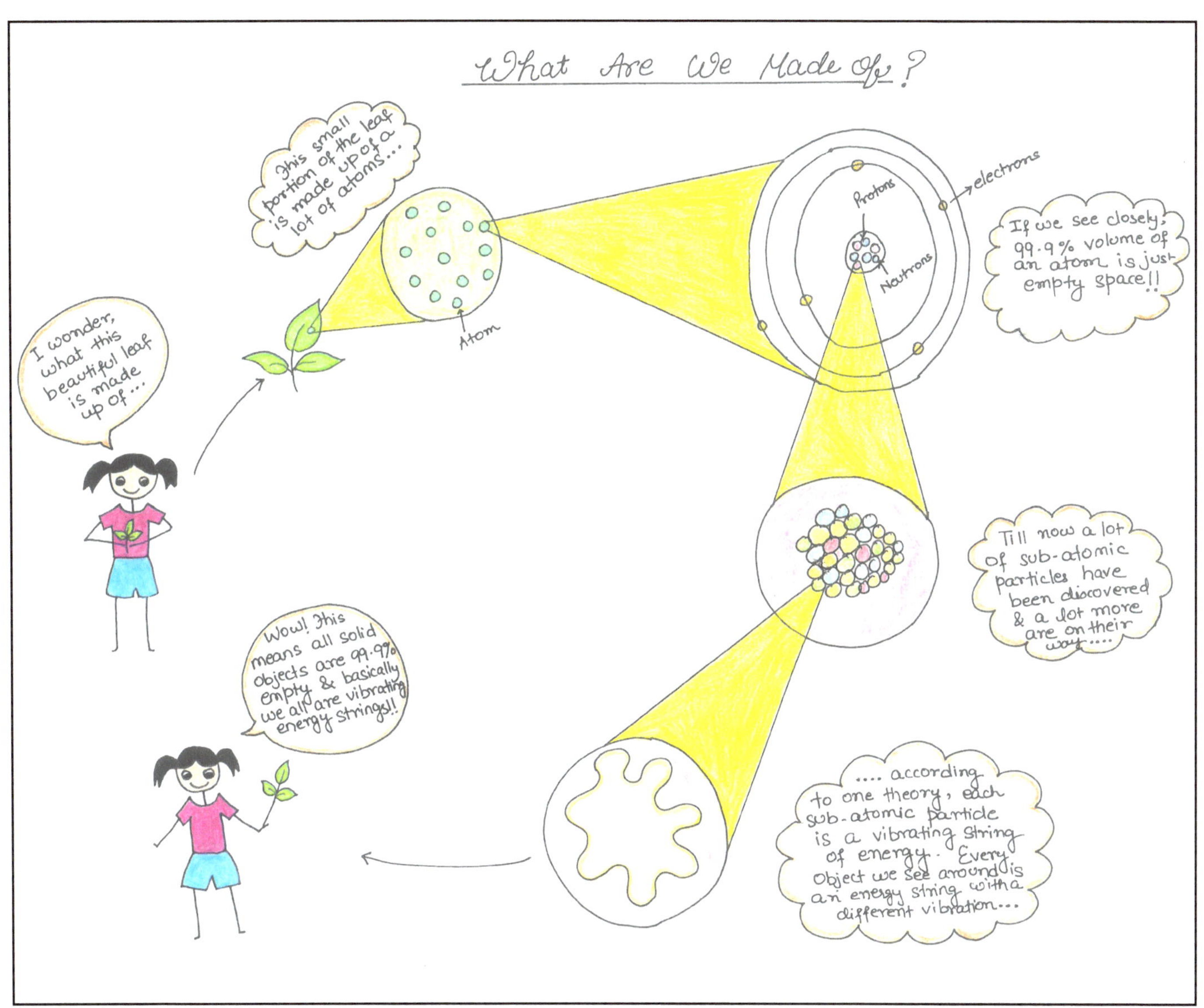
What Are We Made Of?
This small portion of the leaf is made up of a lot of atoms...
Atom
Protons
electrons
Neutrons
If we see closely, 99.9% volume of an atom is just empty space!!
I wonder, what this beautiful leaf is made up of...
Till now a lot of sub-atomic particles have been discovered & a lot more are on their way....
Wow! This means all solid objects are 99.9% empty & basically we all are vibrating energy strings!!
.... according to one theory, each sub-atomic particle is a vibrating string of energy. Every object we see around is an energy string with a different vibration...

Chapter 2 DEATH

Can any living creature go without eating anything? No. This means a constant supply of nutrition must be provided to all the species in the world to keep them alive. This is a natural process. The species alive today that extract nutrition from other beings, whether plants or animals, will one day die and become responsible for providing nutrition to other species. In this way, the cycle of life continues.

So, death is an essential and fundamental part of life. In other words, it is equally important to die as it is to live. There is nothing wrong or bad about death. It simply means that something no longer exists in the same way that we, living beings, exist.

We know that everything in this universe, including all living things, is made up of energy, and we also know that energy can neither be created nor destroyed. Therefore, anything or anyone can never be destroyed; we simply transform into another form of energy and continue to be a part of this beautiful cosmos. That's it.

Death → Beginning of new life

PART 3

AWARENESS

Chapter 1

TAMSO MA JYOTIRGA-MAYA

'Tamso Ma Jyotirgamaya' – In Sanskrit this means to move from darkness towards light, from ignorance towards awareness.

What does ignorance mean? Ignorance simply means not knowing, not understanding. But not understanding what? There are a million things that we don't understand. Yes, we need to know and acknowledge this fact every moment of our lives: we do not know everything in this universe. We can never know everything in its totality in our lifetime. We are a speck in this vast universe. We are small and insignificant compared to the creation around us. That clearly means that even if we have created some technologically advanced equipment and stuff, we have not created the whole universe. Something much, much, much bigger than us is present here. A higher power, a much larger force, is present which is driving everything.

Being aware of this fact and accepting that 'WE DO NOT KNOW EVERYTHING' will free us from our own made-up theories about ourselves. Being humble and realizing the immensity of nature is what awareness is.

तमसो मा ज्योतिर्गमया॥

Chapter 2
EMBRACE IMPERMA-NENCE

When I was a little girl, I had this cute little doll. I used to play with it all day. But slowly, it started to wither away. Its hair began to fall out, and its limbs came off. Nevertheless, I continued to play with it every day, and one fine day, it gave out. I was so upset; I didn't want it to change at all. I cried so much. My father tried to fix it for me, but no matter how hard he tried, he couldn't make it like new. It had 'Changed' permanently.

A similar thing happened again when I grew a little older. My best friend in the whole world moved to a different city. The initial days were very tough for me. I couldn't sleep, couldn't eat, and I didn't want to go to school at all. But slowly, I came to terms with it. I made some new friends and started new hobbies. My life 'Changed'.

Over the years, I have encountered this 'change' many more times. At first, it is always a shock. But slowly, and sometimes painfully, I understood that nothing in this world is permanent. Everything, and I mean literally everything, is impermanent. I truly thank the Almighty for this because it means sad moments are not permanent, and it means bad experiences are not permanent.

As you can see in the picture below, life as we know it is evolving because nothing is permanent, nothing is stuck in one place. Everything is subject to change. The more quickly we accept this, the easier our lives will be.

Chapter 3

TRUE DESIRE

In our day-to-day lives, we desire many things. Sometimes we attain them, and sometimes we don't. It's true that when we don't get what we desire, we often become sad. However, it's also true that after we acquire, use, and enjoy those things, we still end up feeling sad.

Do you ever wonder why this happens? I'll tell you why. It's because we are capable of experiencing much more than just physical comforts. These physical pleasures can keep us engaged for a short span of time only. We all have the capacity to connect with and become one with the vast creation around us. Our bodies and minds inherently understand this, they are designed for this. So, even if we continually seek to indulge in our physical desires, we never truly find lasting happiness.

Believe me, we all have the ability to experience life on at a deeper level, and when we exercise that ability, we come out stronger and happier.

Chapter 4

ORIGIN

Do you wonder where you came from? Yes, your parents, that's right. But where did your parents come from? Yes, you are right again, their parents. But where did their parents come from? From where did their parents come from? This can go on forever until the single-celled organisms, as we all know from evolutionary biology. But the question still remains. From where did that single-celled organism come from? You can see that no matter how hard we try to find the origin of a species, we end up with another species. But if the beginning of all species is another species or living organism, then there has to be another living organism behind it. So, where does it all end? Where do all physical beings, including us, originate from? We do not know the answer yet for sure. But one thing is sure: it cannot be anything physical. It has to be something that is not physical in nature, something beyond that. If that 'something' is the origin of us all, then we can surely call it the 'Almighty,' the 'Creator'... to whom we all constantly crave to return... knowingly or unknowingly.

The Origin

Chapter 5

POORNA VYASTATA – ULTIMATE ENGAGEMENT

Almost all of us in today's fast and furious lifestyle get overwhelmed by the workload that we have, and on top of that, we are in constant worry about what people around us are thinking about us. Why doesn't somebody like me or why did they say those harsh words to me, and many more things like that. So, although our minds are constantly at work and continuously busy, they are still super distracted, deeply unaware, and tremendously tortured every single day. We are never out of this vicious circle. So, what is the way forward? How can we stop this nonsense once and for all? We have to remind ourselves each day that our time on earth is very limited. We have to leave Earth someday for sure.

So, while we live, we need to find our purpose, our goal, the one thing that we dearly love to do, and the one thing that we are passionate about. The thing that will make us stop caring about the nonsense of the world. You have to understand that whatever you choose to do – if it is not giving you inner peace, if it is not relieving you from the baseless chatter of your mind, if it is forcing you to look in anticipation all the time for the validation of the world, then you need to ponder over your choices again. That choice will give you inner peace and meaning to your life only if – it is not centred around the collection of more physical pleasures and fame. It has to be something that is meant for the well-being of life around you. Then you will see how well you are living, how free you are living. Nothing can put a shackle on your feet. You are born free, and you will live free always.

Chapter 6

RASTA - THE WAY

Have you ever seen people around you struggling to get more marks in exams, more money, bigger houses, bigger cars, more power, etc., etc.? I am sure you and I also want such things in life. I would be lying if I said no. But have you ever wondered that even after getting all that they want, they are never truly happy, never truly satisfied, and constantly want even more? So, what is it that we actually want? It is definitely not these physical pleasures and fame. We have already got enough proof of that from our surroundings. Then what is it that we actually want?

Maybe we want the biggest possibility in life. What can be the biggest and most powerful? A wealthy business person? No...because there can always be a wealthier business person. So, a best sports person, or an engineer... no, there can always be someone better. Nobody can be the best always. So, the question still remains – what is the biggest possibility?

The biggest possibility does not only mean to become big, but to become infinite. But everything physical will always be finite, no matter how much in quantity it is. It will aways have a limit.

So, can we become infinite in any way? I do not know yet. But what I know is that we can choose a path that can lead to the infinite. And that the path, as we have understood, doesn't go through wealth or intelligence. That path is a path of pure love and compassion.

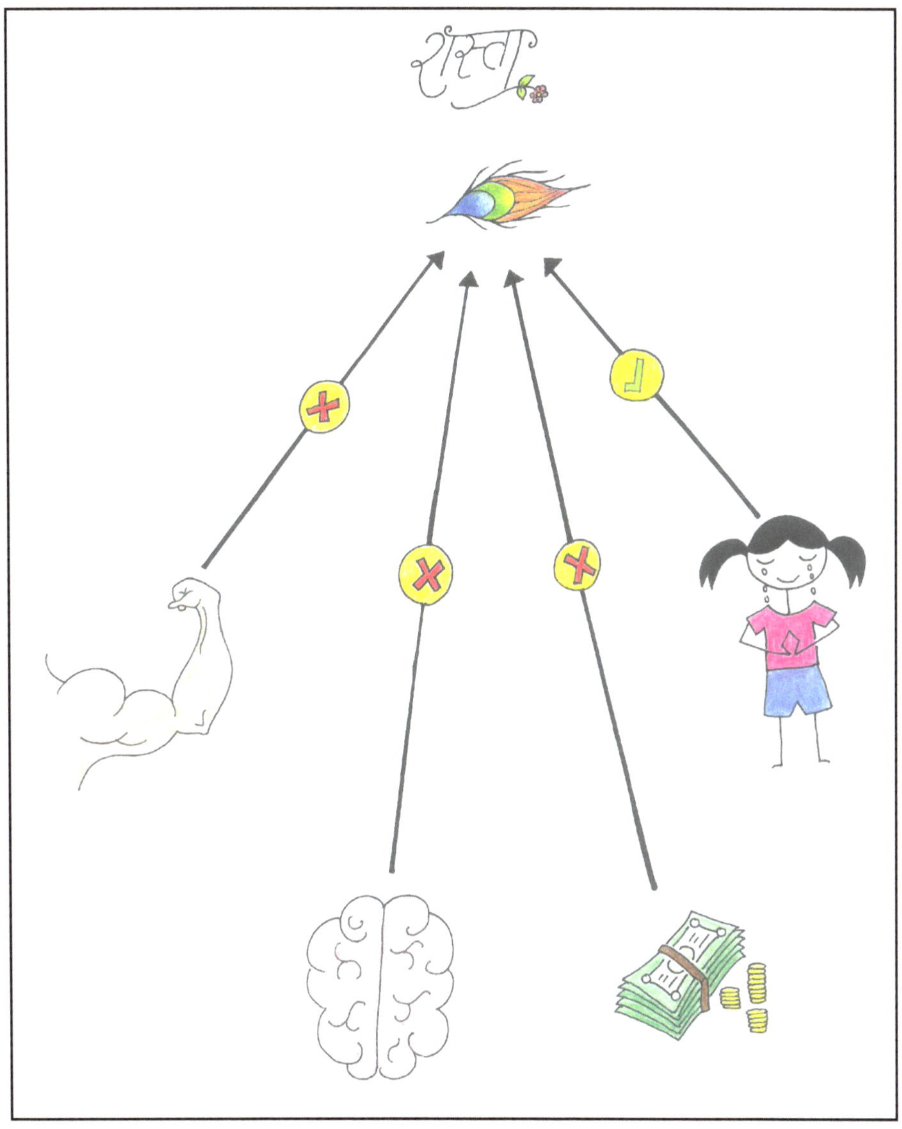

PART 4

ACTIONS

Chapter 1

TOGETHER WE ARE STRONG

For generations, the modern man has always considered himself the superior being and believed that all other species are only created for his consumption. This thinking has caused catastrophic damage to all the flora and fauna including human beings themselves. Our society is infected with even bigger diseases than the recent pandemic – racism and capitalism, to name a few.

Dear friends, you must know that you are the future of mankind. You have the chance to rectify the damage. You must understand that this false feeling of superiority that has plagued the minds of human beings is our enemy. This is the reason that day by day, more and more people, especially young people, are under the grip of severe mental health issues. This is one major factor that is crippling our society. In such an environment, nobody can thrive, and ultimately, we will meet our doom sooner than expected.

So, do not care what people around you are up to. You need to start your journey to create an 'all-inclusive' space of your own. You have to remind yourself that all life is precious, and all of us are unique.

Nobody should be disrespected just because they look different from you, lead a different life from you, or have fewer opportunities or commodities than you.

Let's join hands and vow to make Earth a beautiful place to live again, a place where everyone is treated alike.

Chapter 2

A GOOD LIFE

What does a good life look like? Just look back and think about the last time you got a toy or a gadget. How long did it keep you happy? Or think about that dress you bought. How long did that keep you happy? Now, think about that friend you had or still do, with whom you have shared your life at one time, or that dog you kept as a pet, or the time when you shared your chocolate with that less fortunate kid at that railway station.

Now, compare both the feelings you had just now, about that dress and your friend. Which one brought a warm feeling to your heart? The quality of one's life is determined by the experiences one has. If all those experiences are anxiety, jealousy, anger, and depression, then it surely is a wasted life. You have been given this one precious life, my friends...

Please go and have more and more fulfilling experiences that do not give you temporary joy but a joy that will last a lifetime.

A GOOD LIFE
Money Oriented
Love Oriented
Actions
Actions
N
DONATION
Result
Result
1. Anxiety
2. Jealousy
3. Anger
4. Dipression
5. Hatred
1. Health
2. Joy
3. Love
4. Peace
5. Success

Chapter 3

SOLDIERS OF THE EARTH

It would be foolish to think that we are running our lives alone. Our lives are possible because numerous factors are playing their role perfectly, without which we can't even survive for a minute. The trees, the birds, the insects, and the animals, all are making our life on Earth possible. The birds and insects are responsible for pollination, due to which we can have all our fresh fruits and veggies. The animals are also helping in agriculture. Even the faeces of animals or the decaying parts of a tree are making the soil richer, on which life can grow to the fullest. All the life around us is deeply connected to each other in some way or the other.

Human beings are often quoted as the 'Most Intelligent' beings on the planet. But look around you. Do you see intelligence or stupidity? The rising global warming, the pollution, the violence... all are proof that we are not that intelligent after all. We have done immense damage to our Mother Earth. But now it is high time that each one of us takes the responsibility of taking care of our only home and becomes 'Soldiers of the Earth.'

SOLDIERS OF THE EARTH
SAVE WATER
REDUCE POLLUTION
EAT PLANTS NOT MEAT
PLANT MORE TREES
LOVE ANIMALS

Chapter 4

NEVER GIVE UP

"Dear friends, always remember that with a heart full of love and passion, there is nothing in this world that you can't achieve. There are numerous examples of great people who showed us how. Below, I have briefly outlined a few of my favourite idols.

1. **Dashrath Manjhi –** The great Dashrath Manjhi, also known as the Mountain Man, belonged to a tribal class in Jharkhand. He was a labourer in Gehlaur village, near Gaya in Bihar, India. The poor people of that village had to climb a mountain to reach the other side to collect drinking water. On a fateful day, he lost his wife on the same mountain. His wife died in the year 1959 due to an injury caused by falling from this mountain, and due to this obstacle, he was not able to reach the hospital in time. That day, this man decided to cut open that mountain and make an easy roadway for the villagers so that nobody else would suffer such an unfortunate death. This man worked alone relentlessly for 22 years (1960-1982) and succeeded. He manually carved the mountain to connect Gehlaur and Gaya. His work was later recognized and rewarded by the

then Chief Minister of Bihar. In 2016, the Indian Post issued a postage stamp featuring him. He carved a path 110 m long, 7.7 m deep in places, and 9.1 m wide to form a road through the ridge of rocks. He said, "When I started hammering the hill, people called me a lunatic, but that steeled my resolve." This man, Mr. Manjhi, was extremely poor, a common man with no extraordinary abilities, as some might say. But look at what he accomplished with a heart full of love and passion for the entire society.

2. **Arunima Sinha** – Arunima is the first female amputee to climb Mount Everest. She was a national-level volleyball player. On 12th April 2011, she was traveling from Lucknow to Delhi via train. On her way, some goons tried to snatch the gold chain that she was wearing. They were not successful in snatching the chain from her, and they pushed her out from the running train. The moment she fell on the tracks, another train came and went over her left leg. She lost her leg. The right leg was also badly injured, and she had multiple spinal cord fractures. After a long treatment of 4 months in Delhi, she got back her life. But now she was treated differently. She had two choices – either to give herself away from depression and lock herself away from the world or to fight, and she chose to fight. She vowed to climb Mount Everest. After she was discharged from the hospital, she went straight to Bachendri Pal, the first female in India to climb Mount Everest. Arunima started her training with her. She faced immense difficulties, but she stood undeterred. After two years of rigorous training, she successfully climbed the highest mountain in the world on 21st May 2013. After climbing Mount Everest, Arunima Sinha's next goal was to climb all the seven highest peaks in all seven continents.

She covered six peaks, i.e., in Asia, Europe, South America, Australia, Africa, and North America by the year 2014. On 4th January 2019, she climbed the seventh peak on Antarctica and became the world's first female amputee to climb Mount Vinson. Arunima Sinha is living proof that no matter how hard or how impossible the situation around you seems to be, you should NEVER GIVE UP.

3. **Sindhutai Sapkal –** Sindhutai Sapkal was a social worker and social activist known for her work in raising orphaned children in India. She was born into a poor family in Maharashtra. Due to poverty, she was forced to quit school and was married off at the age of 12 to a man 20 years older than her. She had a difficult marriage and left home at the age of 20, with a girl child in her arms. She started begging for food at railway stations. During that time, she realized that there were a lot of children abandoned by their parents. She started to take care of those children. She begged vigorously not just for herself but for all the other children that she adopted. She decided to become a mother to everyone who came across her as an orphan. Later, Sindhutai fought for the rehabilitation of tribal villages in the district of Chikaldara, situated in the Amravati district of Maharashtra. These villages were evacuated for a tiger preservation project. She took care of many Adivasi children and treated them as her own. Sindhutai devoted herself to these orphans. They fondly called her 'Mai'. She nurtured over 1,500 orphaned children and through them had a grand family of 382 sons-in-law and 49 daughters-in-law. She has been honoured with more than 700 awards for her work. She used this award money to buy land for making a home for the orphaned children.

These great beings have shown us the path. They have proved that no matter how hard the goal seems to be, if you have a deep love for what you are doing and you strongly believe in the cause, nothing in the world can stop you.

Chapter 5

GOING HOME

Leaving this fake, materialistic world behind, let us start moving towards our true nature. Let us strive to be the humans that the Creator created with so much love. Use every means and every ounce of your energy to reach your true potential because we have very limited time on Earth.

We must make use of every second of this precious life to add more meaning and create a difference for all life around us.

GOING HOME

EPILOGUE

They say that being born as a human is the greatest gift of nature. Human's intellect relieves them from living the life of an animal and gives them sophistication and culture. But, there is a catch. It takes a whole lot of work to develop as a 'Human Being'. Just being born as a human does not qualify one for any privileged category, and it does not give anyone the right to harm the life around them. Unfortunately, very few people understand this. Majority of us start our lives with ignorance and end it with ignorance.

Nature has worked really hard to bestow us with all the prowess that we have today - an agile body, and a sharp mind. With such sophisticated machinery, living the life of an ignorant but sophisticated 'Animal' is a great misfortune. If we want to make use of this human life and tap into its full potential, we have to make the journey from Ignorance to Awareness.

This book is a humble attempt to give you a glimpse of the mistakes we make in our daily lives because of our limited understanding and ideologies. It is also an endeavour to show a path of clarity that can help you come out of those mistakes and make better use of this rare, one-time opportunity of 'Being Human'.

All Inclusive.

ABOUT THE AUTHOR

Ankita Sen Kundu is a chemical engineer working for a petrochemical company. She also holds an MBA degree in human resources. She is from Kolkata, West Bengal. She is currently residing with her family in Surat, Gujarat, where she works.

Ankita is a mental health advocate, a spiritual seeker, an avid reader, a blogger, and an illustrator. She is very passionate about conveying deep thoughts in the simplest forms so that not only children, but adults too can grasp the true essence of these learnings and make their lives meaningful.

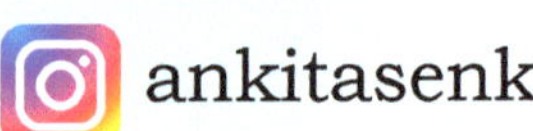

www.ingramcontent.com/pod-product-compliance
Lightning Source LLC
LaVergne TN
LVHW070300170826
845679LV00031B/651

* 9 7 9 8 8 9 2 7 7 8 3 0 5 *